PIANO SOLO

MANNHEIM STEAM R

T0041086

Romantic Melodies

ISBN 0-634-05607-7

DOTS AND LINES, INK

9130 MORMON BRIDGE ROAD OMAHA, NEBRASKA 68152 402.457.4341

EXCLUSIVELY DISTRIBUTED BY

HAL•LEONARD®
CORPORATION
7777 W. BLUEMOUND RD. P.O. BOX 13819 MILWAUKEE, WI 53213

Visit Hal Leonard Online at
www.halleonard.com

CONTENTS

SERENITY
from IMPRESSIONS

By CHIP DAVIS

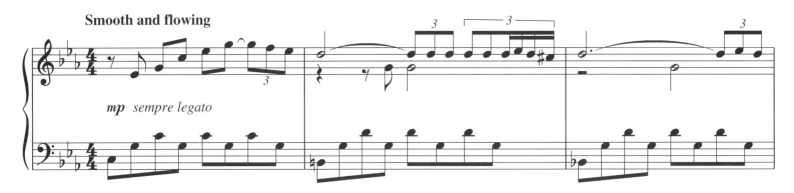

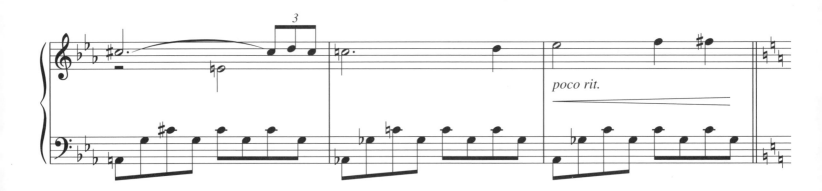

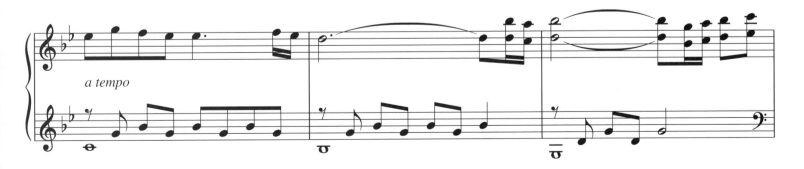

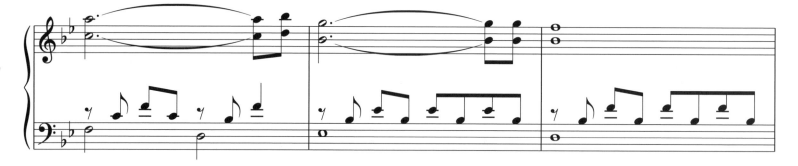

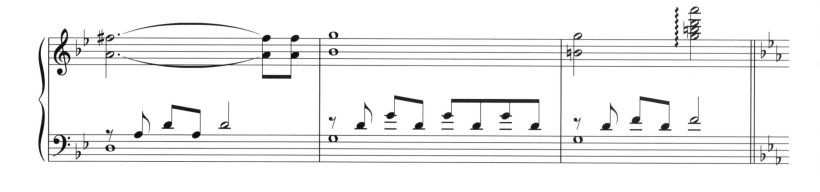

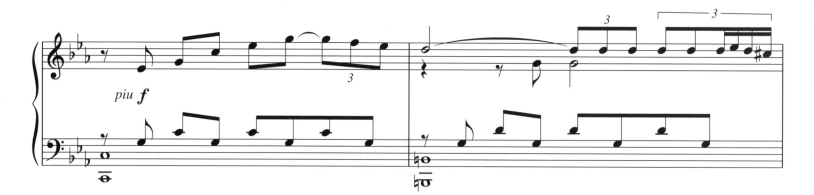

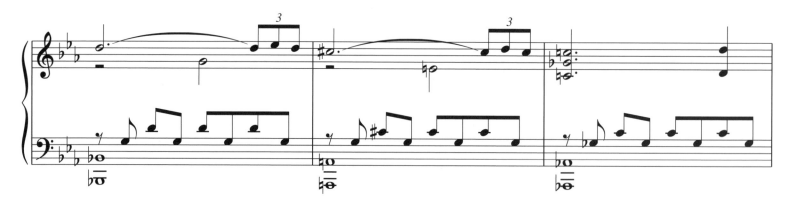

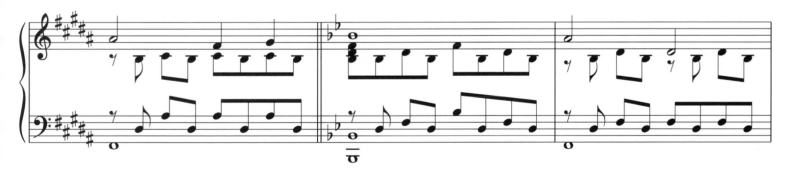

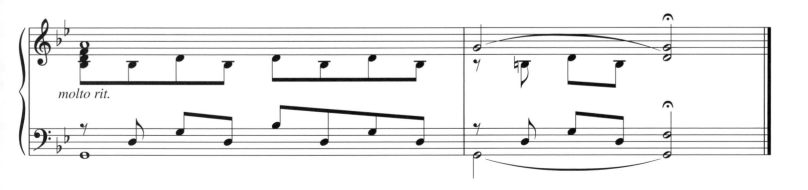

SUNDAY MORNING BREEZE

from SUNDAY MORNING COFFEE II

By CHIP DAVIS

To Coda

D.S. al Coda

CODA

BITTERSWEET
from SUMMER SONG

By CHIP DAVIS

Slowly

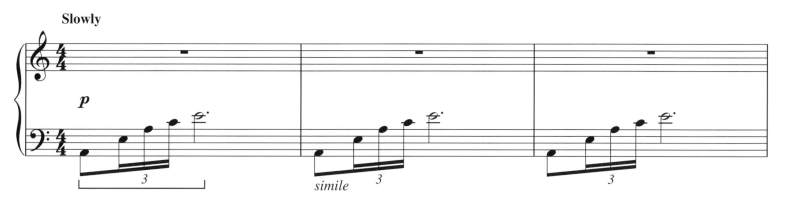

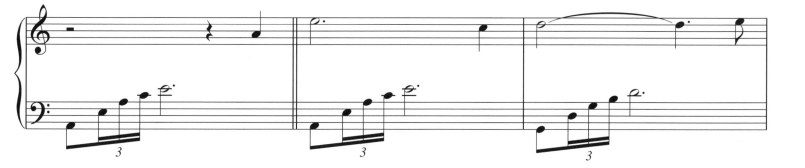

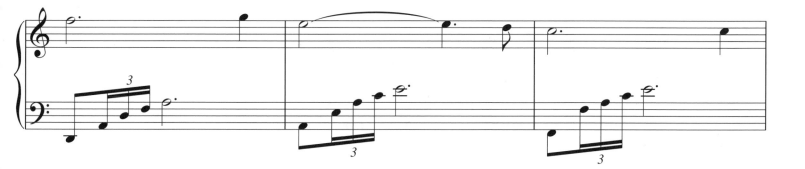

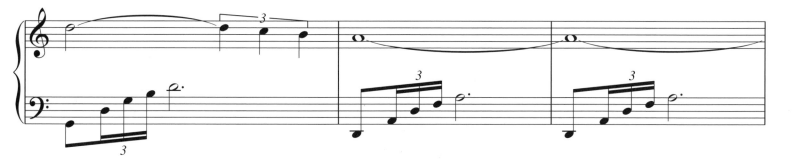

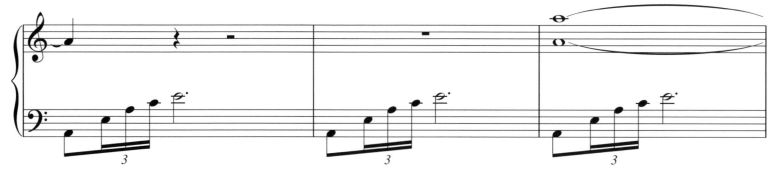

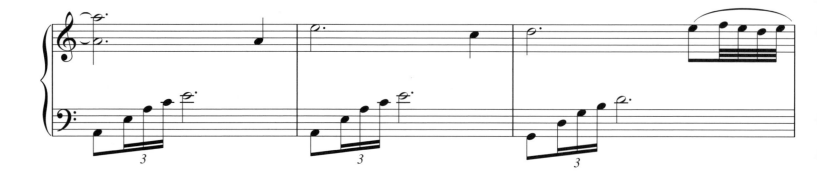

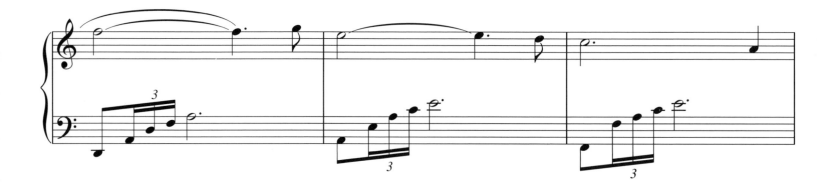

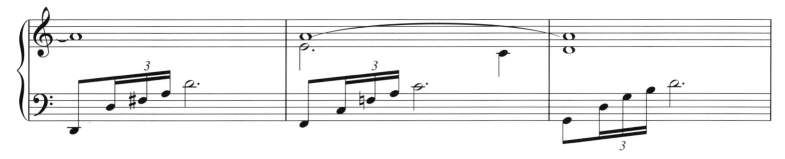

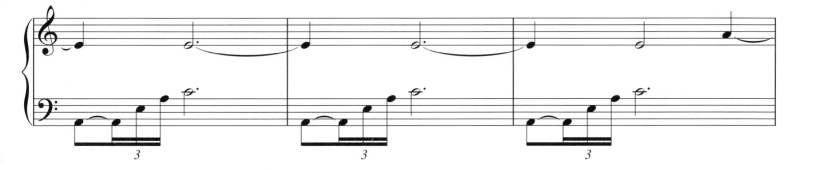

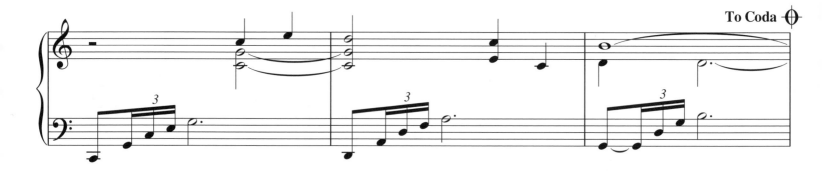

To Coda ⊕

mf

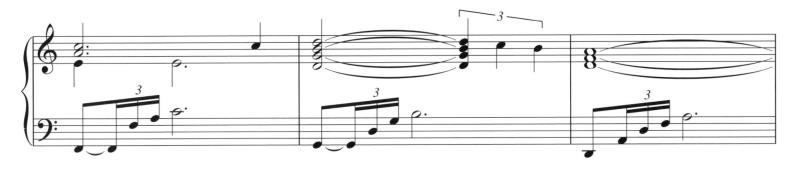

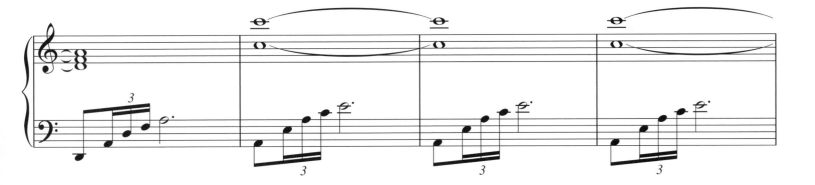

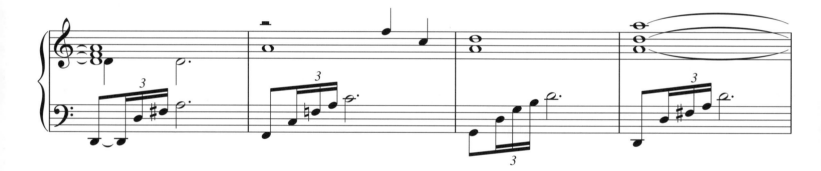

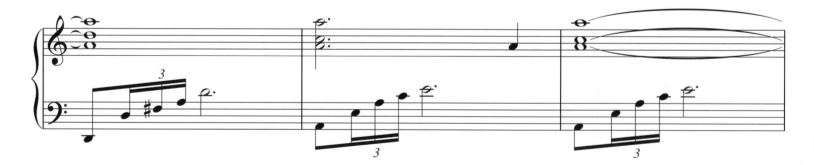

D.S. al Coda

CODA

mf

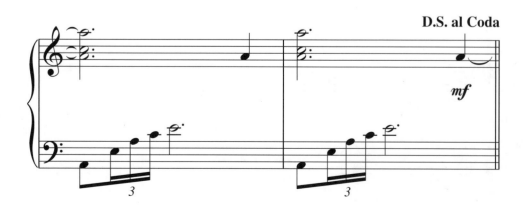

SLO DANCIN' IN THE LIVING ROOM

from ROMANCE II

By CHIP DAVIS

Slow and smoothly (♩ = 60)

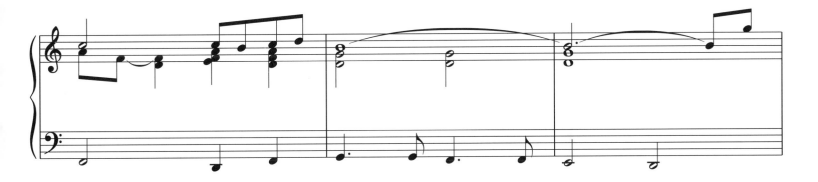

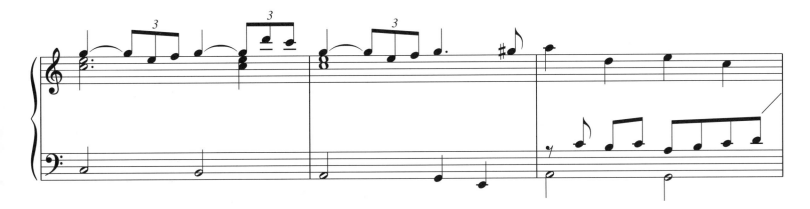

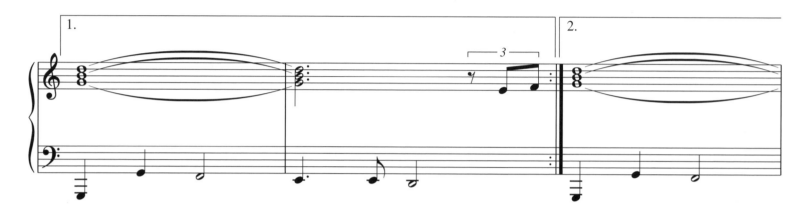

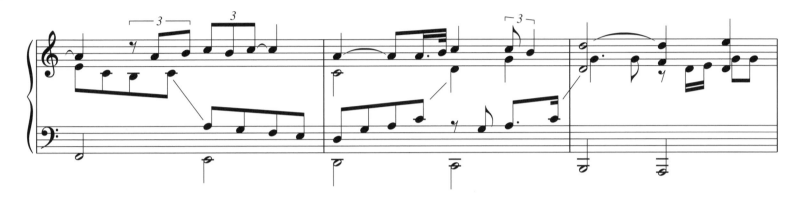

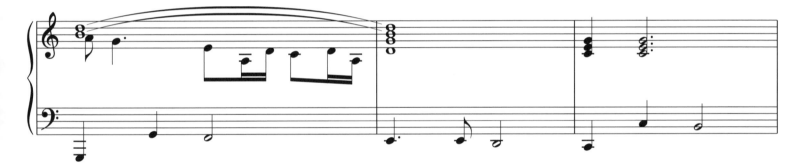

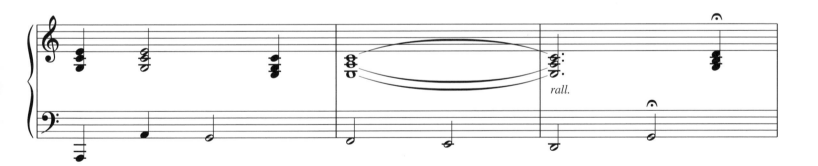

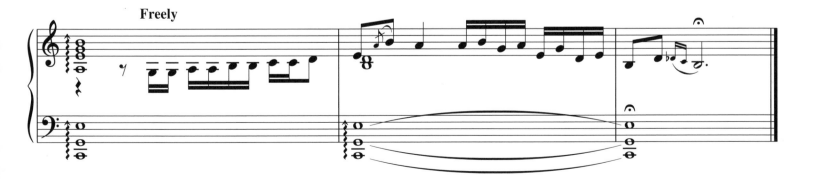

KANBAI
from ROMANCE

By CHIP DAVIS

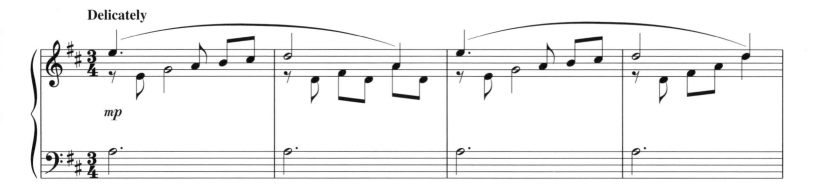

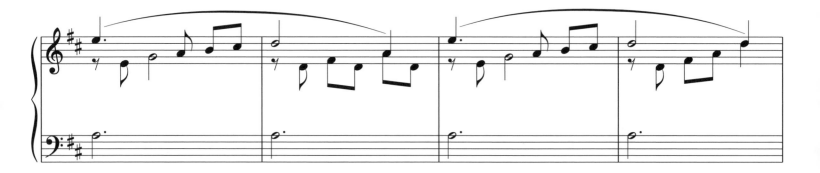

Last time To Coda ⊕

D.C. al Coda
(with repeat)

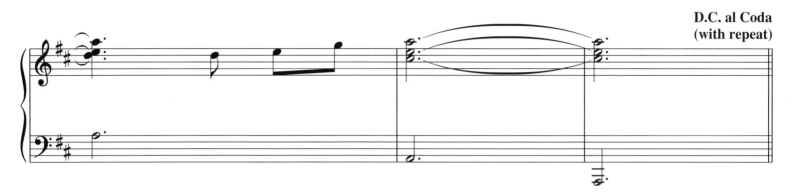

CODA

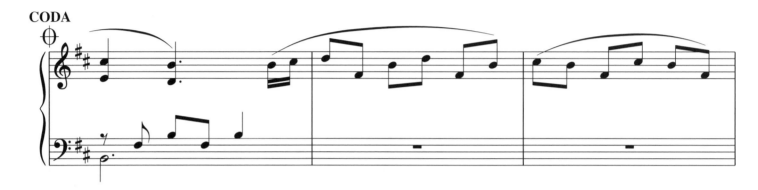

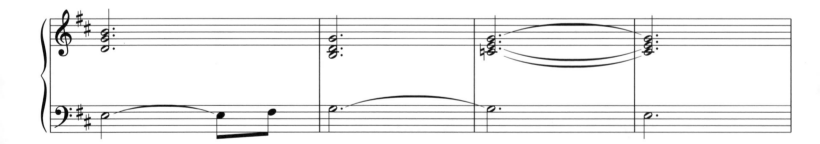

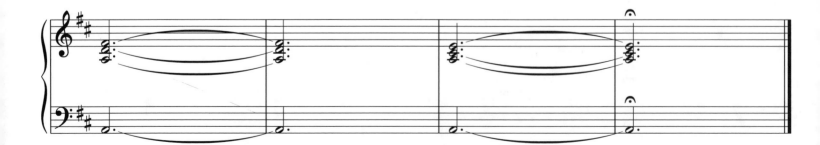

THE SIGN OF LOVE

from IMPRESSIONS

By CHIP DAVIS

Lyrical and expressive

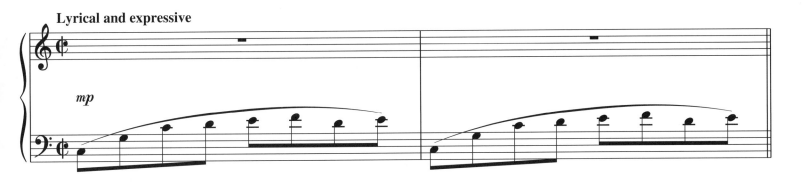

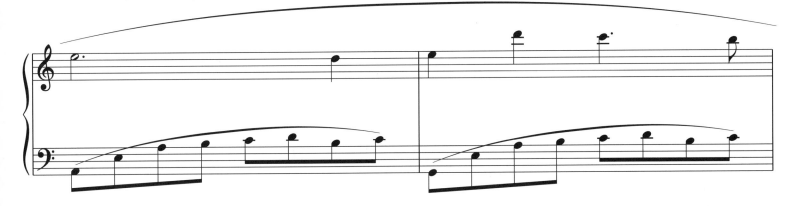

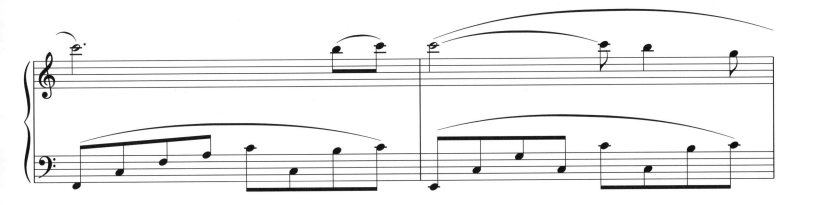

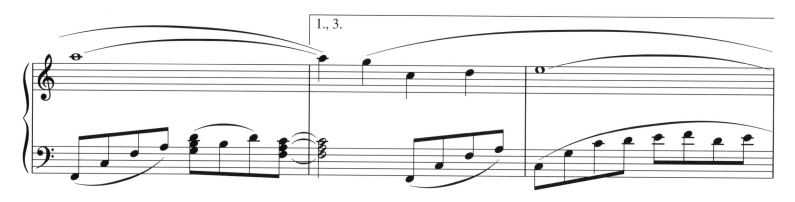

1., 3.

2., 4.

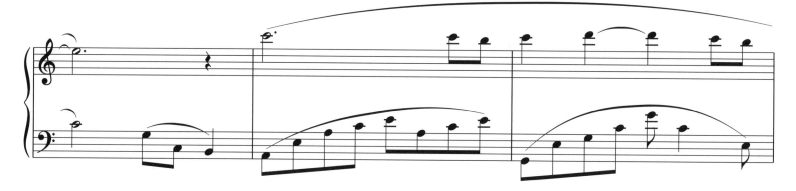

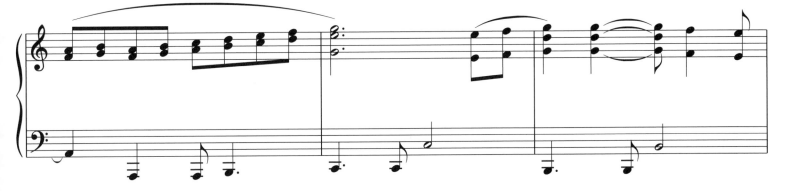

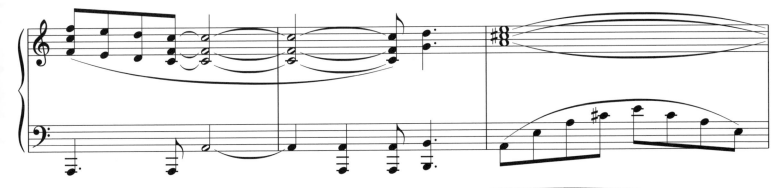

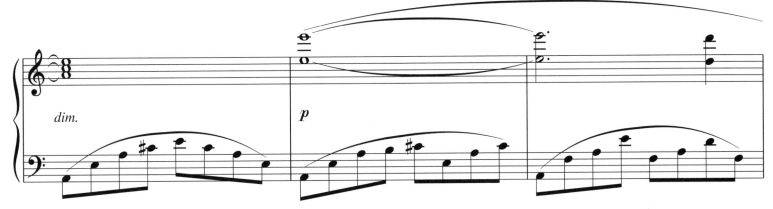

28

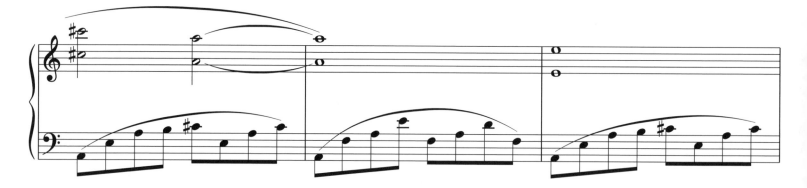

To Coda ⊕

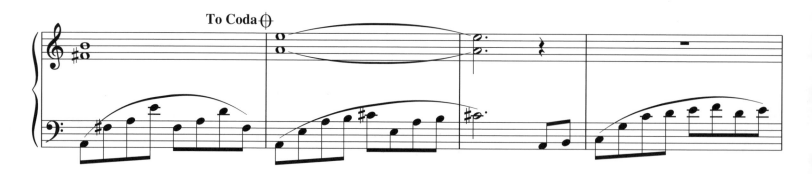

D.S. al Coda
(with repeat)

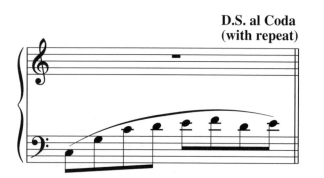

CODA
⊕

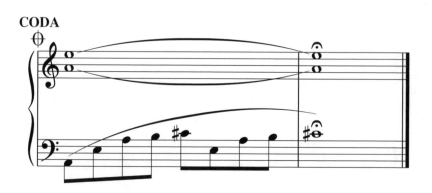

TEARDROPS RAINDROPS
from SUMMER SONG

By CHIP DAVIS

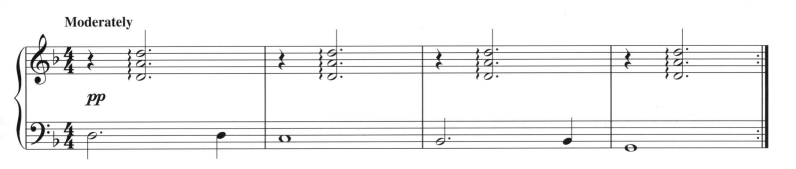

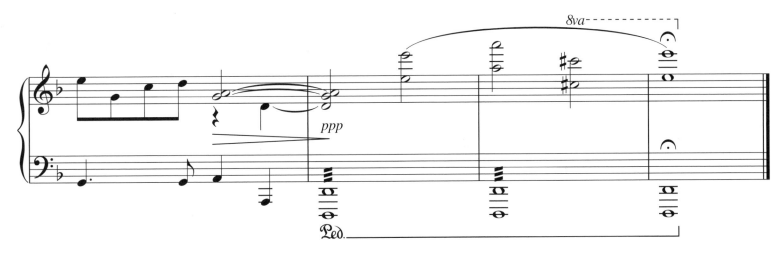

CHAKRA IV
from FRESH AIRE 7

By CHIP DAVIS

Slowly

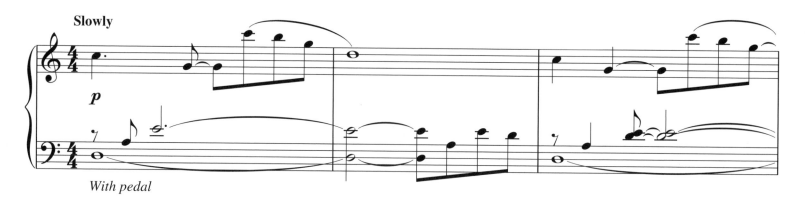

With pedal

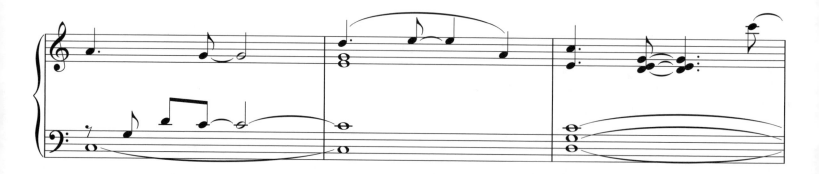

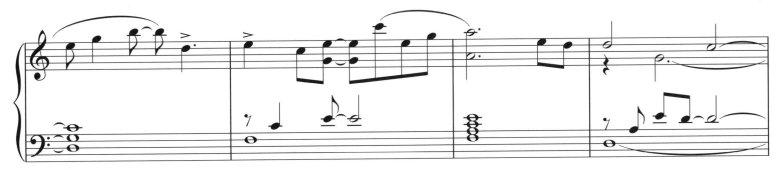

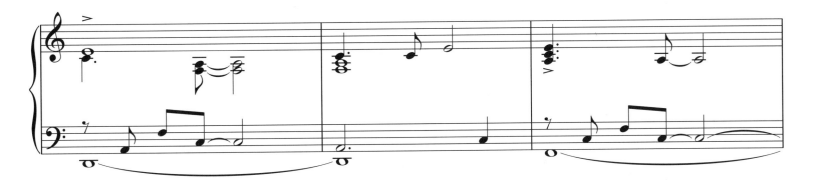

D.C. al Coda

CODA

mf

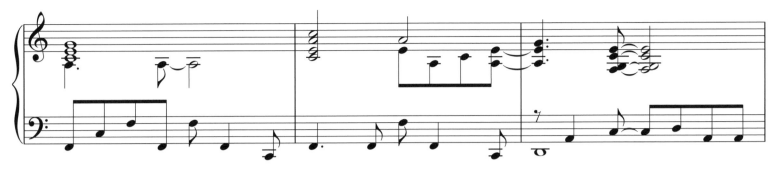

Repeat and Fade

Optional Ending

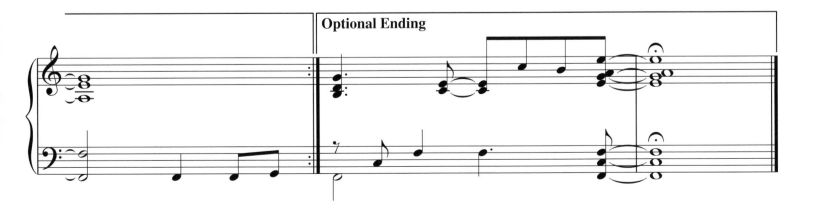

AMBER
from FRESH AIRE III

By CHIP DAVIS

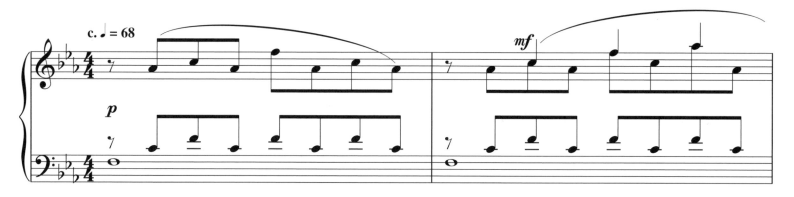

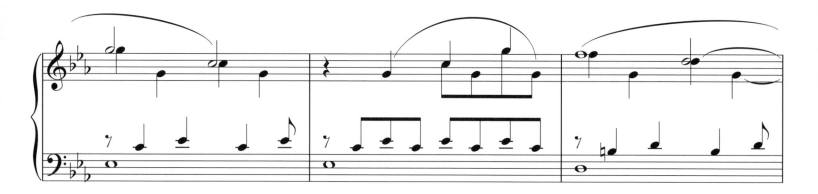

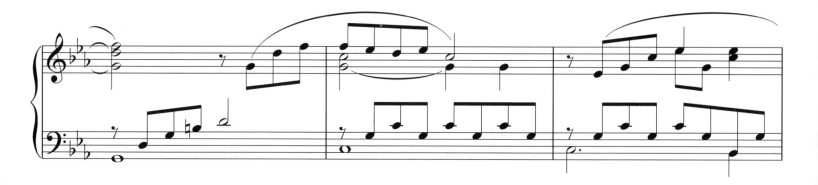

THE 7 STARS OF THE BIG DIPPER

from FRESH AIRE III

By CHIP DAVIS

Gently flowing

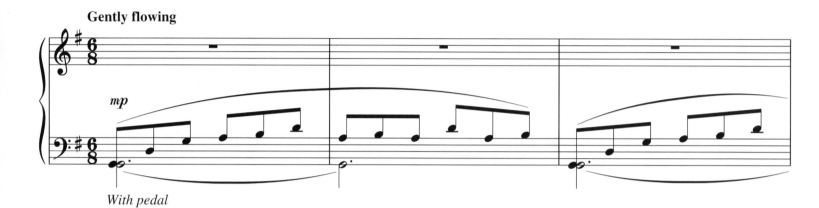

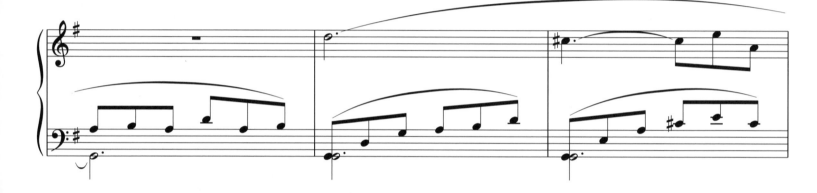

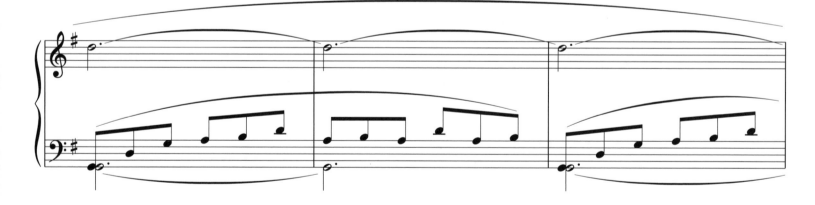

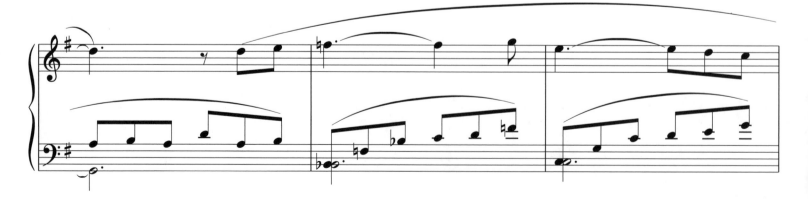

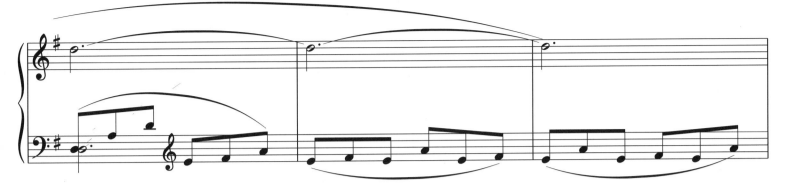

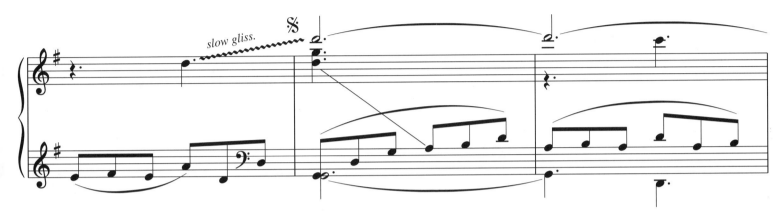

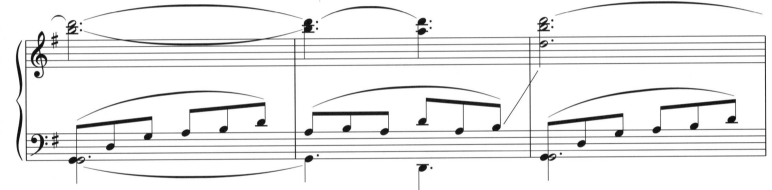

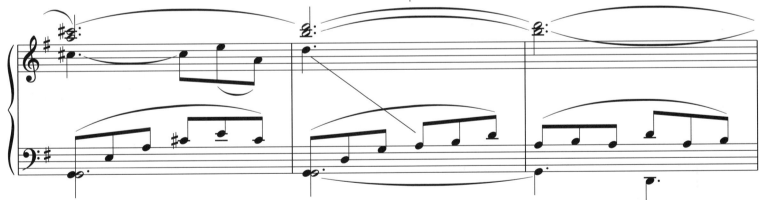

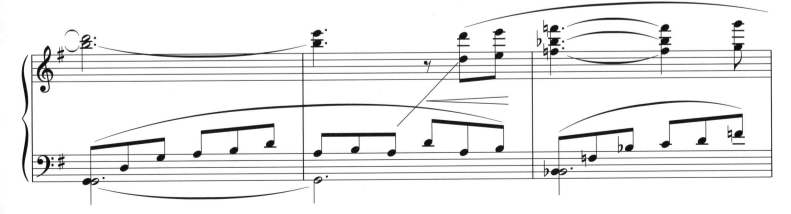

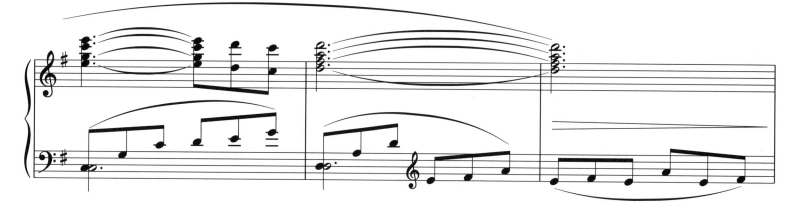

To Coda ⊕

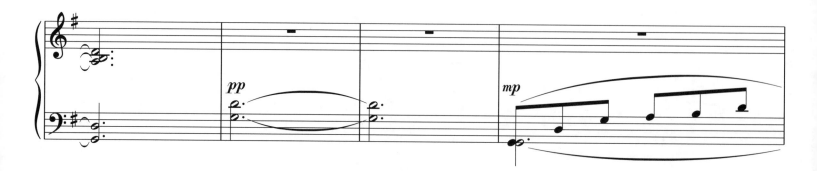

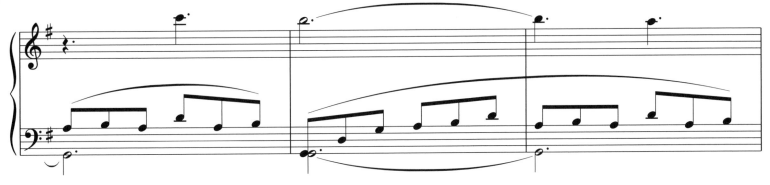

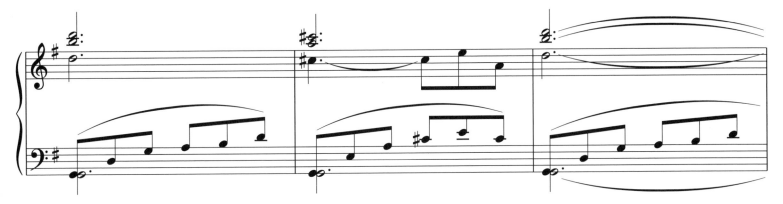

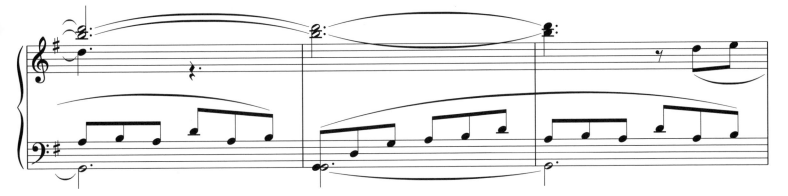

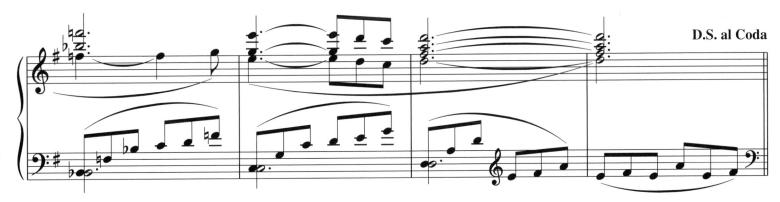

D.S. al Coda

Repeat and Fade

CODA

MOONLIGHT AT COVE CASTLE
from ROMANCE II

By CHIP DAVIS

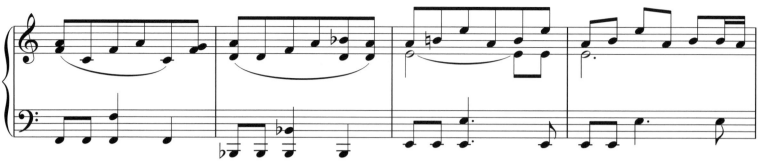

Slower ♩ = 69

NEPENTHE
from FRESH AIRE VI

By CHIP DAVIS

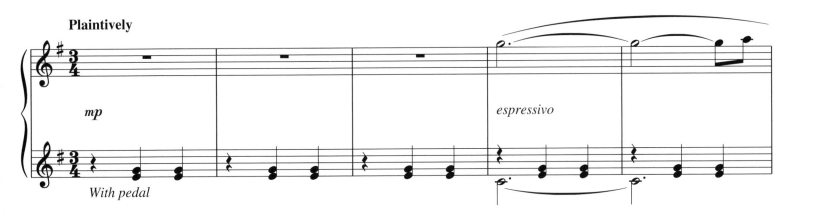

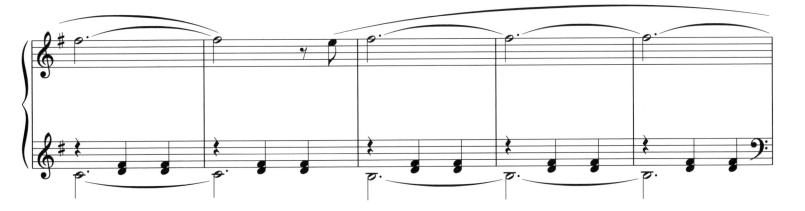

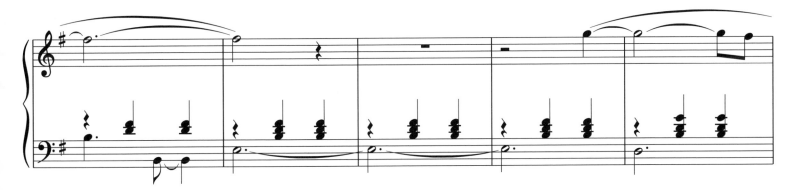

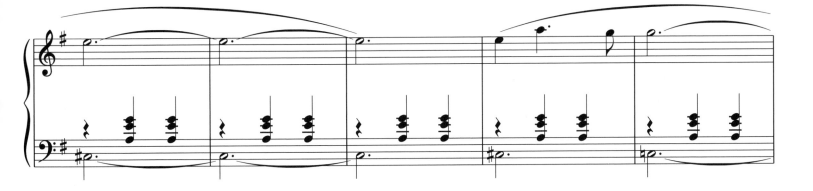

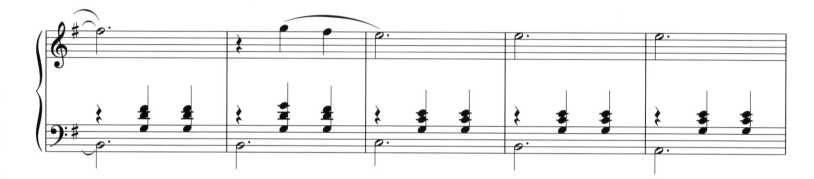

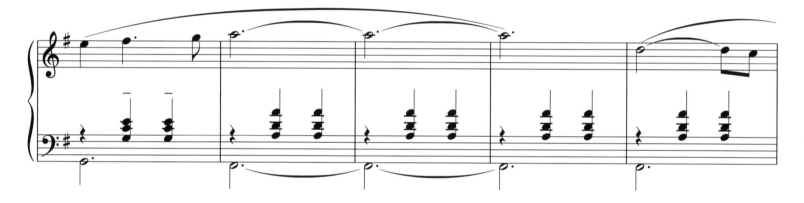

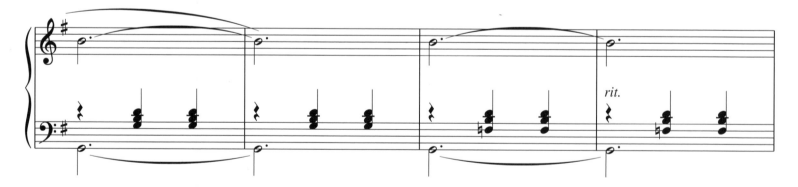

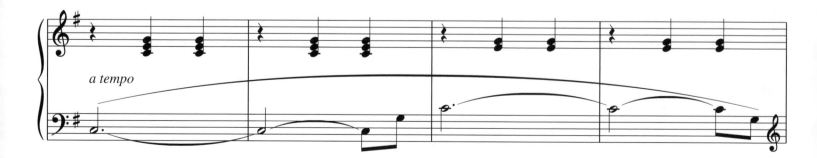

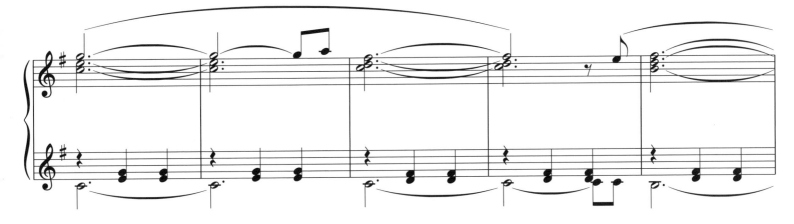

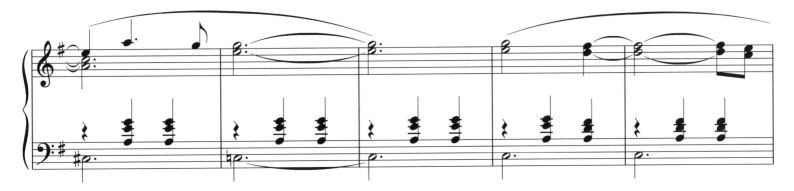

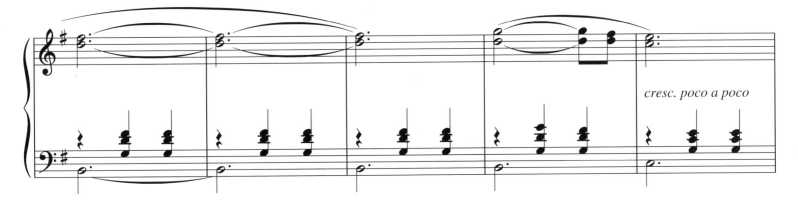

cresc. poco a poco

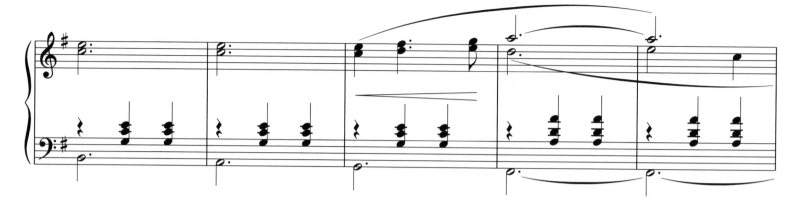

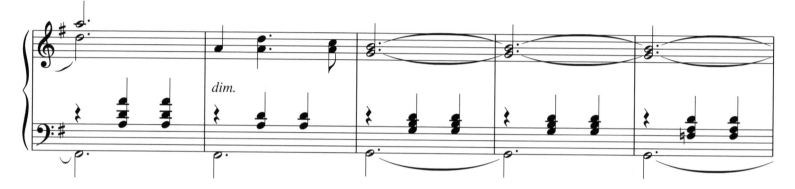

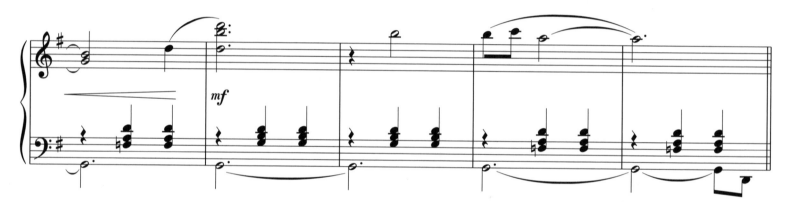

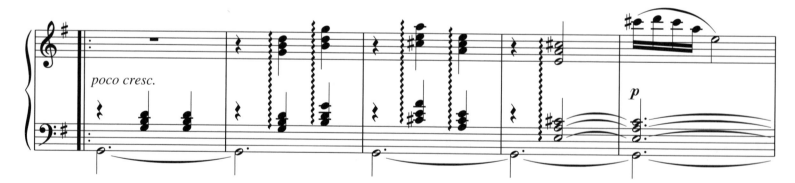

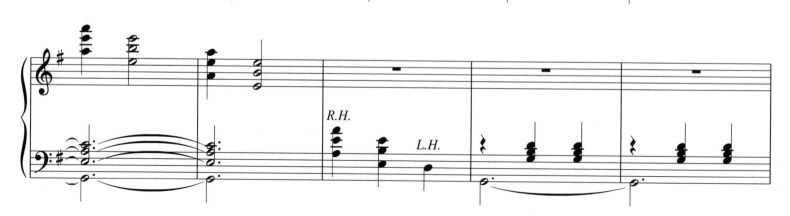

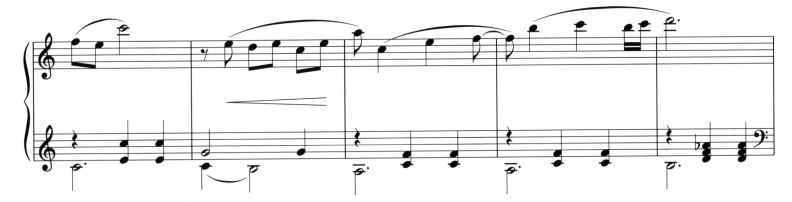

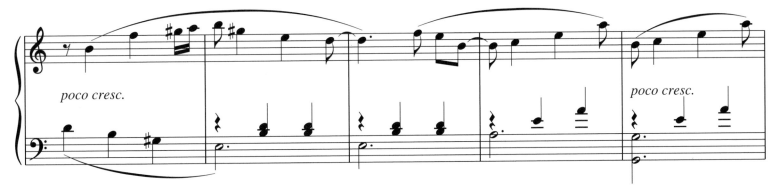

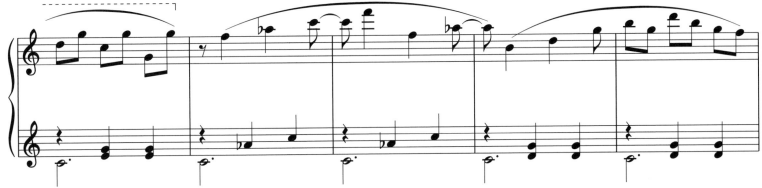

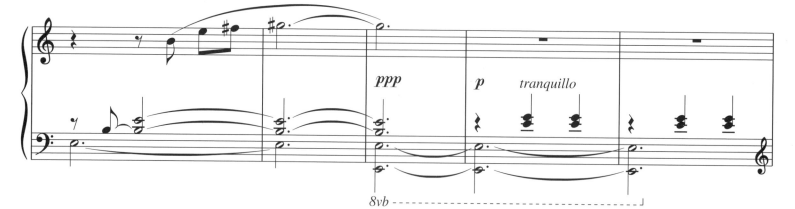

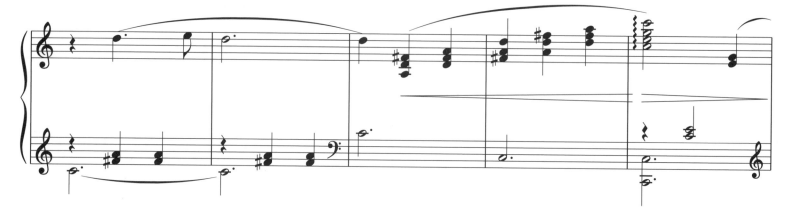

Repeat and Fade